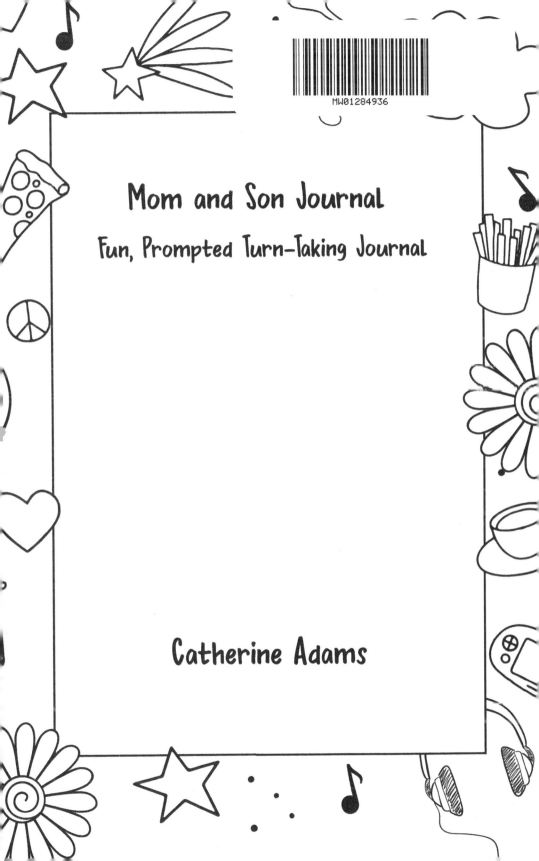

Mom and Son Journal

Fun, Prompted Turn-Taking Journal

Catherine Adams

To awesome Moms who are always try-
ing to improve their family relationships
and to awesome sons who love us enough
to go along with it. (:

Thank you for your purchase - I truly
hope you enjoy this book!

Please let me know your thoughts by
leaving a review on Amazon.com.

Reviews are a big help to me as a small
publisher and they help other customers
as well!

Instructions

1. Have Fun!

2. Activities can be done in any order, so start in the beginning or jump around.

3. Any questions can be answered by discussing out loud, or by taking turns writing or drawing.

4. Give each other permission to skip questions, only do 1 per day or just play tic tac toe!

5. Use the blank pages at the end to come up with your own questions.

6. Quality time spent together is a gift that lasts a lifetime - Enjoy!

Mom answer

This is my son

His full name is

_____

I call him

_____

Son answer

This is my mom

Her full name is

_____

I call her

_____

Mom answer

Create a fun new middle name
that describes your son

_____

_____

_____

_____

_____

INSPIRATION

soccer-boss clever sweetie easy-going animal-loving
cake eating   cell phone-toting   energetic curious caring
book-lover master gamer   fearless-eater   math-wizard
crazy   cutie-pie optimistic sneaker-wearing always-singing
basketball-allstar fast-as-lightning lovable silly brave loved
bestest   creative helpful funny determined sweetheart
patient snuggle-bunny ninja

Son answer

Create a fun new middle name
that describes your mom

_____

_____

_____

_____

_____

INSPIRATION

home-boss smart easy-going animal-loving
coffee-drinking cell phone-toting energetic curious caring book-lover multi-tasking mind-reading chocolate-loving
optimistic legging-wearing always-singing dancing-allstar
fast-as-lightning lovable silly brave loved master-chef creative helpful funny determined sweetheart patient awesome hugging lost and finder ninja

Just for fun

PLAY ROCK, PAPER, SCISSORS

Best of 7 rounds wins

ROUND	WINNER	
	SON	MOM
1		
2		
3		
4		
5		
6		
7		

Mom answer

Your son woke up this morning with one of the following traits. Check which you think will be his top two choices:

_____ Amazingly Athletic

_____ Incredibly Handsome

_____ Crazy Smart

_____ Super Popular

_____ Musically Gifted

What trait would you choose for him? Why?

_____
_____
_____
_____
_____
_____
_____
_____
_____

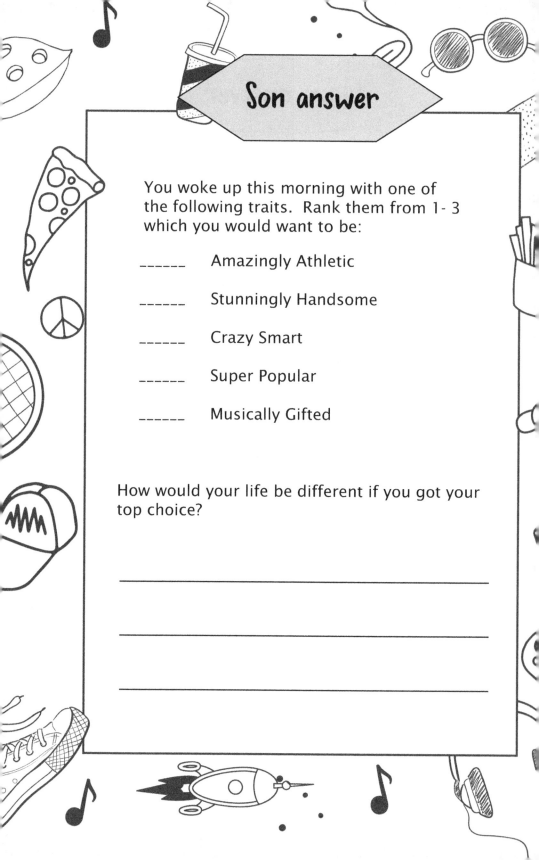

You woke up this morning with one of the following traits. Rank them from 1- 3 which you would want to be:

_____   Amazingly Athletic

_____   Stunningly Handsome

_____   Crazy Smart

_____   Super Popular

_____   Musically Gifted

How would your life be different if you got your top choice?

_____

_____

_____

We answer/discuss

After you both have answered, discuss or write why you chose the traits you did or if you were surprised by each others choices:

_____

_____

_____

_____

_____

_____

_____

_____

_____

Just for fun

Congratulations

You are now the
Supreme Ruler of Earth
and you may solve one world problem
today. What will it be?

_____ Disease

_____ War & Terrorism

_____ Climate Change & Pollution

_____ Poverty & Starvation

_____ Drug & Substance Abuse

Place a check mark on the right to predict
your son's choice.

Congratulations

You are now the
Supreme Ruler of Earth
and you may solve one world problem
today. What will it be?

_____ Disease

_____ War & Terrorism

_____ Climate Change & Pollution

_____ Poverty & Starvation

_____ Drug & Substance Abuse

Place a check mark on the right to predict
your mom's choice.

We answer/discuss

After you both have answered, discuss or write why you made the choice you did. What would have been your second choices?

_____

_____

_____

_____

_____

_____

_____

_____

_____

Just for fun

Dots and Boxes

Take turns connecting 2 dots by drawing a line between them. When you draw the last line of a single box, put your initial in it, and make the next move. Player with the most boxes wins.

Mom answer

When you were little where was the scariest place in your room?

_____   Under the bed

_____   In the closet

_____   Outside the window

_____   Somewhere else?

What did you think was hiding? What did you think would happen?

_____
_____
_____
_____
_____
_____
_____
_____
_____
_____

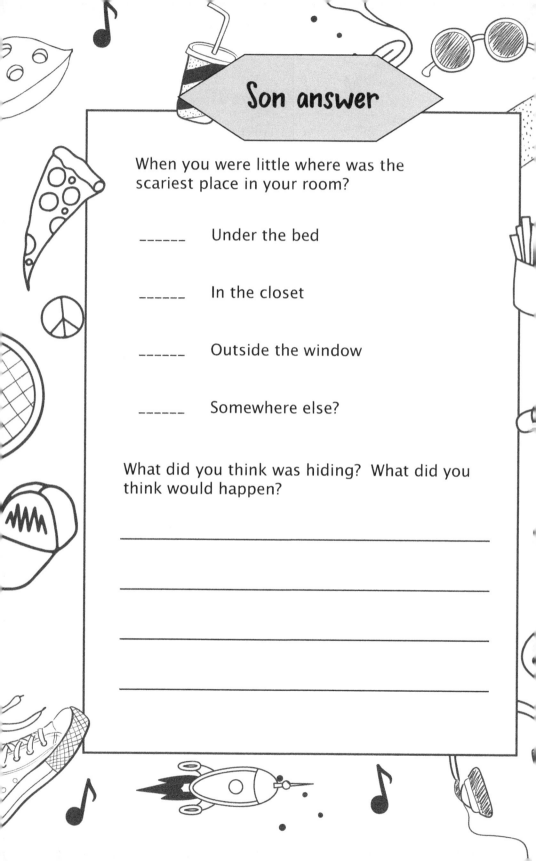

Son answer

When you were little where was the scariest place in your room?

_____   Under the bed

_____   In the closet

_____   Outside the window

_____   Somewhere else?

What did you think was hiding? What did you think would happen?

_____

_____

_____

_____

We answer/discuss

Did you tell anyone about your fears? Do you still fear something in your room sometimes? Mom, tell or write about a time when you were scared for your son.

_____

_____

_____

_____

_____

_____

_____

_____

Just for fun

Mom answer

What 2 things are you the most worried about regarding your son right now?

_____

_____

What 2 things are you the most worried about regarding your son in the future?

_____

_____

Name one thing in your sons life that you think he is the most worried about right now:

_____

Who worries more about his life? (circle one)

I do   He does

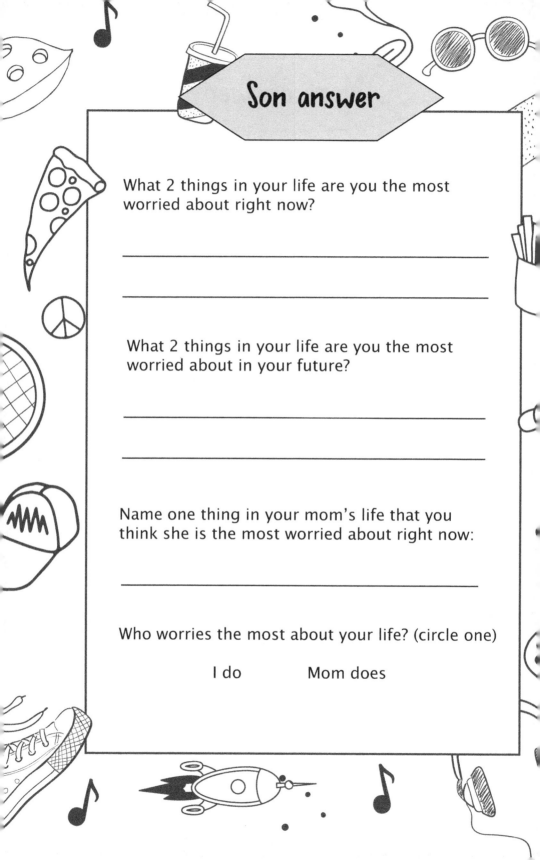

Son answer

What 2 things in your life are you the most worried about right now?

_____

_____

What 2 things in your life are you the most worried about in your future?

_____

_____

Name one thing in your mom's life that you think she is the most worried about right now:

_____

Who worries the most about your life? (circle one)

I do   Mom does

We answer/discuss

Is there anything you can do about the things you're worried about? Is there anything you can do for each other?

_____

_____

_____

_____

_____

_____

_____

_____

Just for fun

PLAY ROCK, PAPER, SCISSORS

Best of 7 rounds wins

ROUND	WINNER	
	SON	MOM
1		
2		
3		
4		
5		
6		
7		

Mom answer

About School....
This year what subject does your son...

do the best in?

_____

like the most?

_____

like the least?

_____

find the easiest?

_____

find the hardest?

_____

What subject can you help him the most in? The least in?

_____
_____
_____
_____
_____

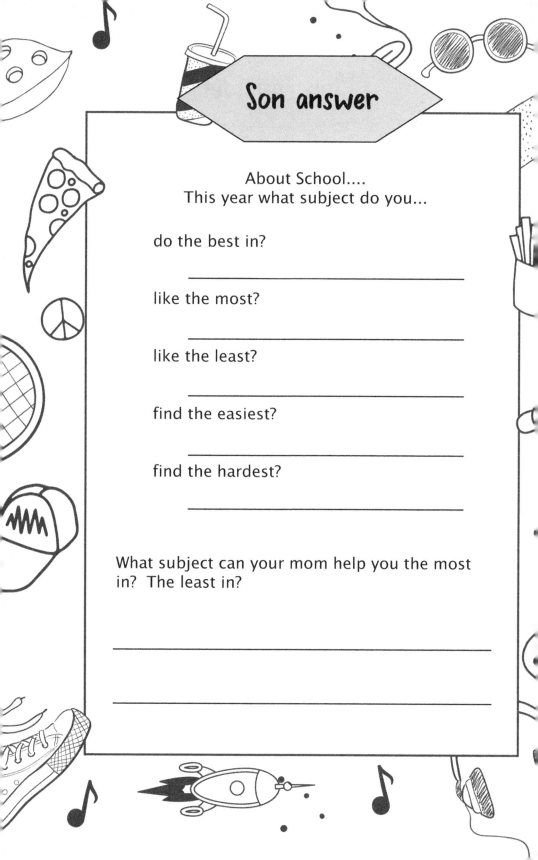

Son answer

About School....
This year what subject do you...

do the best in?

_____

like the most?

_____

like the least?

_____

find the easiest?

_____

find the hardest?

_____

What subject can your mom help you the most in? The least in?

_____

_____

We answer/discuss

Were you surprised by each other's choices? Mom, share what was hardest and easiest for you in school.

_____

_____

_____

_____

_____

_____

_____

_____

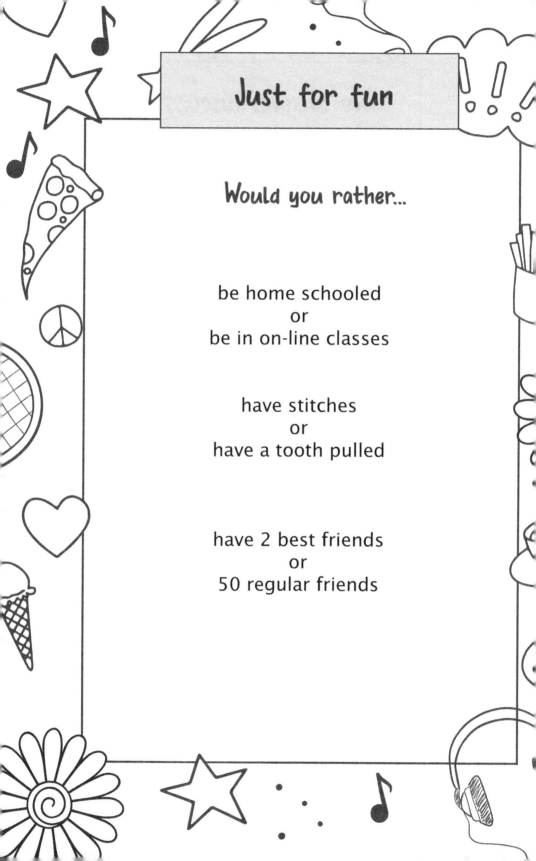

Just for fun

Would you rather...

be home schooled
or
be in on-line classes

have stitches
or
have a tooth pulled

have 2 best friends
or
50 regular friends

Mom answer

Do you believe in ghosts?
yes / no

Why or why not?

_____
_____
_____
_____

Does your son believe in ghosts?
yes/no

Do you believe in aliens?
yes / no

Why or why not?

_____
_____
_____
_____

Does your son believe in aliens?
yes/no

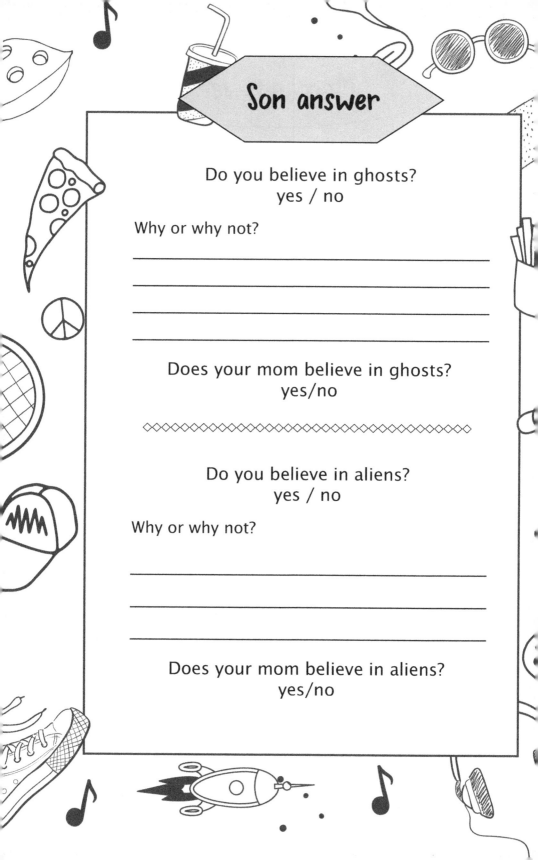

Son answer

Do you believe in ghosts?
yes / no

Why or why not?

_____

_____

_____

_____

Does your mom believe in ghosts?
yes/no

◇◇◇◇◇◇◇◇◇◇◇◇◇◇◇◇◇◇◇◇◇◇◇◇◇◇◇◇◇◇◇◇◇◇

Do you believe in aliens?
yes / no

Why or why not?

_____

_____

_____

Does your mom believe in aliens?
yes/no

We answer/discuss

Have you ever or do you know someone who has had a personal experience with either? Did you believe them? Which one do you hope exists more - ghosts or aliens?

_____

_____

_____

_____

_____

_____

_____

_____

Just for fun

Dots and Boxes

Take turns connecting 2 dots by drawing a line between them. When you draw the last line of a single box, put your initial in it, and make the next move. Player with the most boxes wins.

Mom answer

What two awesome things have you taught your son?

_____

_____

_____

_____

What two things have you learned from your son?

_____

_____

_____

_____

Son answer

What are two things you could teach your mom?

_____

_____

What are the two best things you have learned from your mom?

_____

_____

We answer/discuss

Come up with at least one thing it would be fun for both of you to learn together.

_____

_____

_____

_____

_____

_____

_____

_____

_____

Just for fun

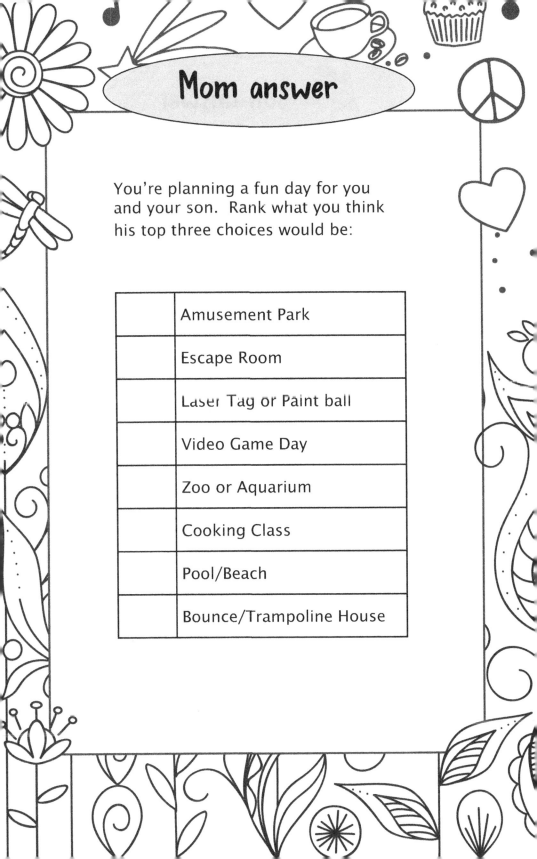

Mom answer

You're planning a fun day for you and your son. Rank what you think his top three choices would be:

	Amusement Park
	Escape Room
	Laser Tag or Paint ball
	Video Game Day
	Zoo or Aquarium
	Cooking Class
	Pool/Beach
	Bounce/Trampoline House

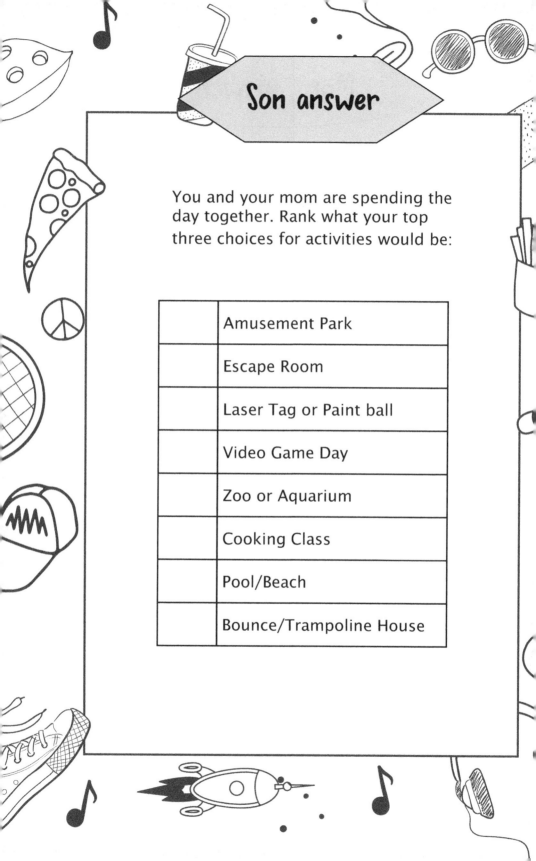

You and your mom are spending the day together. Rank what your top three choices for activities would be:

	Amusement Park
	Escape Room
	Laser Tag or Paint ball
	Video Game Day
	Zoo or Aquarium
	Cooking Class
	Pool/Beach
	Bounce/Trampoline House

We answer/discuss

Mom, what kind of parties did you have or attend at your sons age?

_____

_____

_____

_____

_____

_____

_____

_____

_____

Just for fun

PLAY ROCK, PAPER, SCISSORS

Best of 7 rounds wins

ROUND	WINNER	
	SON	MOM
1		
2		
3		
4		
5		
6		
7		

Mom answer

What 3 positive traits would describe your son?

_____

_____

_____

What are 2 things he does that you appreciate?

_____

_____

What 3 positive traits would describe your mom?

_____

_____

_____

What are 3 things she does that you appreciate?

_____

_____

_____

We answer/discuss

Did your mom/son know what you appreciated about her/him?

_____

_____

_____

_____

_____

_____

_____

_____

_____

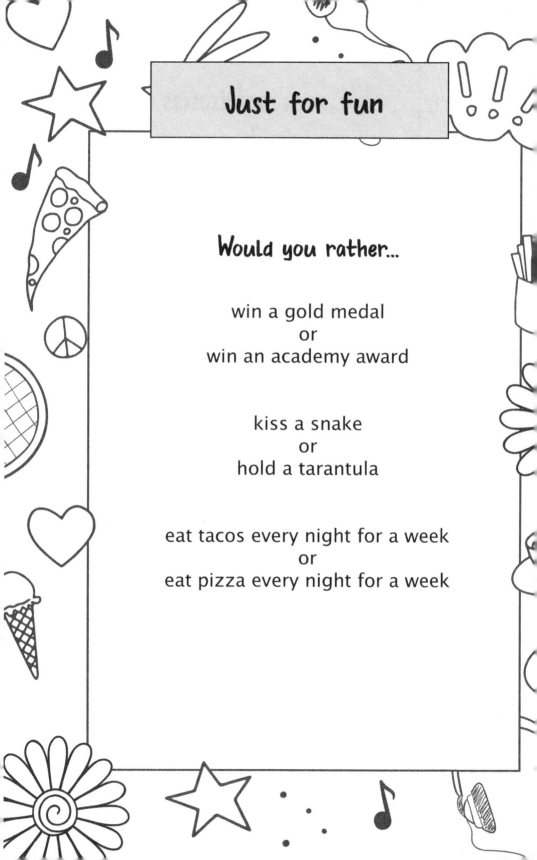

Just for fun

Would you rather...

win a gold medal
or
win an academy award

kiss a snake
or
hold a tarantula

eat tacos every night for a week
or
eat pizza every night for a week

Mom answer

Check 3 things you'd like to do more of with your son:

_____ make dinner/kitchen experiments

_____ play games

_____ have conversations

_____ be active (sports/walks/bike rides...)

_____ go out to lunch or dinner

_____ watch TV/just hang out

_____ play video games

_____ do art/projects/music

_____ go to a live sporting event

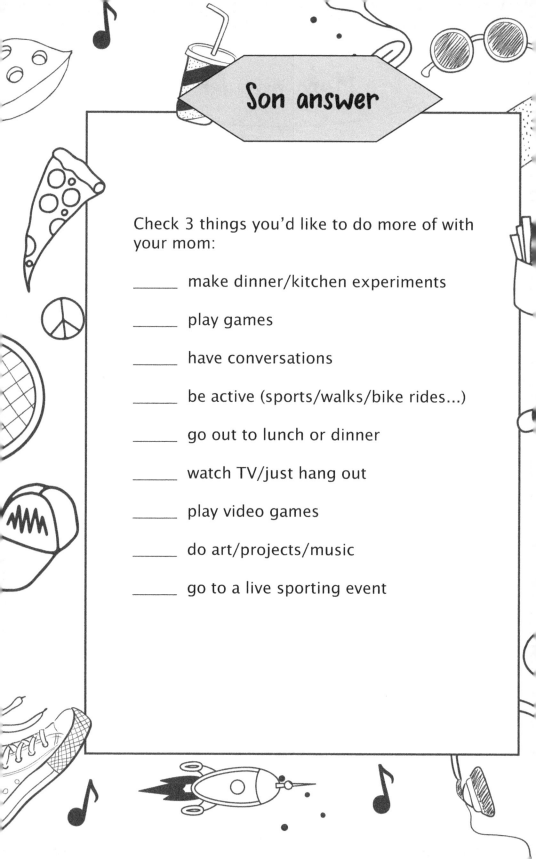

Son answer

Check 3 things you'd like to do more of with your mom:

_____ make dinner/kitchen experiments

_____ play games

_____ have conversations

_____ be active (sports/walks/bike rides...)

_____ go out to lunch or dinner

_____ watch TV/just hang out

_____ play video games

_____ do art/projects/music

_____ go to a live sporting event

We answer/discuss

After you both have answered, agree to do at least one that you both checked sometime in the next week or two.

_____

_____

_____

_____

_____

_____

_____

_____

Just for fun

Would you rather...

live in the clouds
or
under the sea

have really small eyes
or
a really big nose

be rich and sad
or
happy and poor

Mom answer

Hola! Bonjour! Ciao!
Namaste! Salaam!
Ni Hau! Ola! Bula!

You woke up this morning fluent in a new language. What do you hope it is?

_____

Why?

_____
_____
_____

What would you want it to be for your son?

_____

Why?

_____
_____

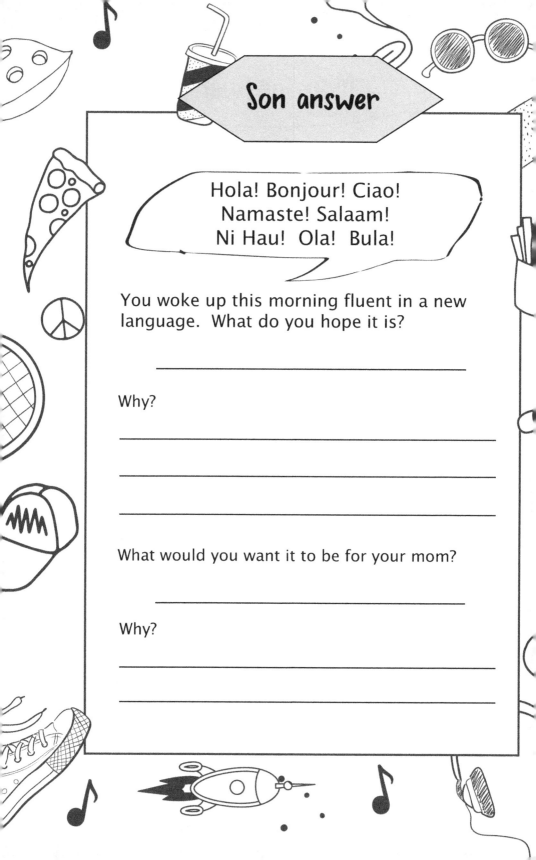

Son answer

Hola! Bonjour! Ciao!
Namaste! Salaam!
Ni Hau! Ola! Bula!

You woke up this morning fluent in a new language. What do you hope it is?

_____

Why?

_____

_____

_____

What would you want it to be for your mom?

_____

Why?

_____

_____

We answer/discuss

What do you think would make the best common world language that everyone would learn as a child? Which of you is better at learning languages?

_____

_____

_____

_____

_____

_____

_____

_____

Just for fun

Dots and Boxes

Take turns connecting 2 dots by drawing a line between them. When you draw the last line of a single box, put your initial in it, and make the next move. Player with the most boxes wins.

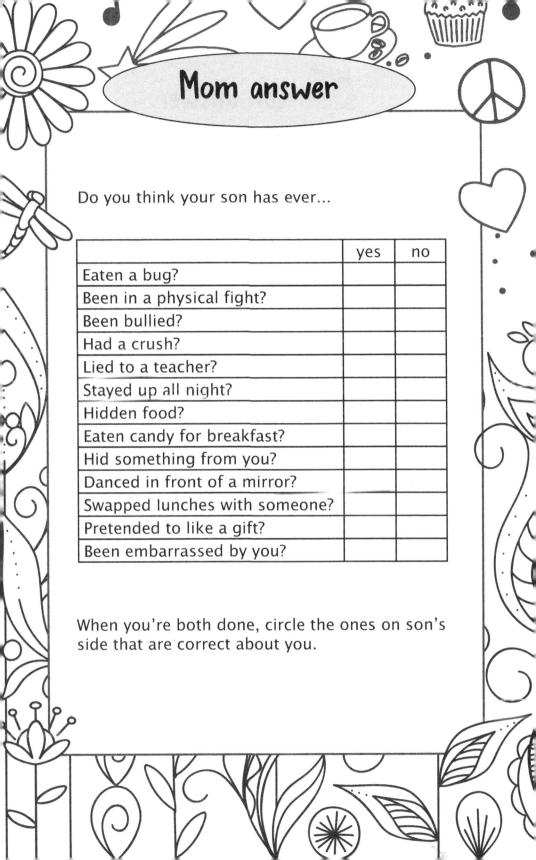

Mom answer

Do you think your son has ever...

	yes	no
Eaten a bug?		
Been in a physical fight?		
Been bullied?		
Had a crush?		
Lied to a teacher?		
Stayed up all night?		
Hidden food?		
Eaten candy for breakfast?		
Hid something from you?		
Danced in front of a mirror?		
Swapped lunches with someone?		
Pretended to like a gift?		
Been embarrassed by you?		

When you're both done, circle the ones on son's side that are correct about you.

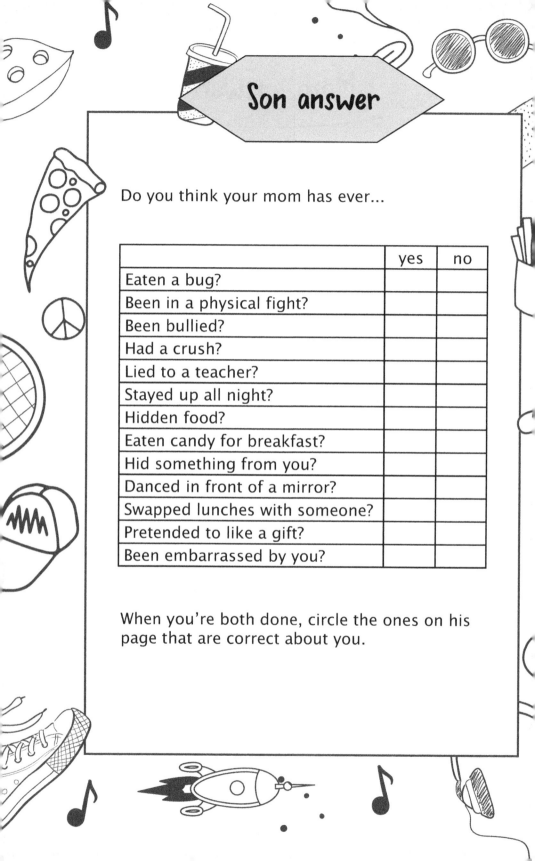

Son answer

Do you think your mom has ever...

	yes	no
Eaten a bug?		
Been in a physical fight?		
Been bullied?		
Had a crush?		
Lied to a teacher?		
Stayed up all night?		
Hidden food?		
Eaten candy for breakfast?		
Hid something from you?		
Danced in front of a mirror?		
Swapped lunches with someone?		
Pretended to like a gift?		
Been embarrassed by you?		

When you're both done, circle the ones on his page that are correct about you.

We answer/discuss

How important is honesty in your relationship?
Is it sometimes okay to lie or to keep a secret?

_____

_____

_____

_____

_____

_____

_____

_____

_____

Just for fun

Mom answer

List 3 things you are proud of your son for this year:

_____

_____

_____

List 2 things you are proud of yourself for this year:

_____

_____

Son answer

List 3 things you are proud of yourself
for this year:

_____

_____

_____

List 2 things you are proud of your
mom for this year:

_____

_____

We answer/discuss

Was is hard or easy to come up with these? What is one thing you wish you could add to your list?

_____

_____

_____

_____

_____

_____

_____

_____

_____

Just for fun

PLAY ROCK, PAPER, SCISSORS

Best of 7 rounds wins

ROUND	WINNER	
	SON	MOM
1		
2		
3		
4		
5		
6		
7		

Mom answer

In your ideal job/career what are the top three things that are most important for you?

_____ Great location

_____ Rewarding/love it

_____ Lots of travel

_____ High income

_____ Great co-workers

_____ Lots of time off

_____ Be my own boss

_____ Makes a difference

Place a check on the right next to the two you think your son will choose.

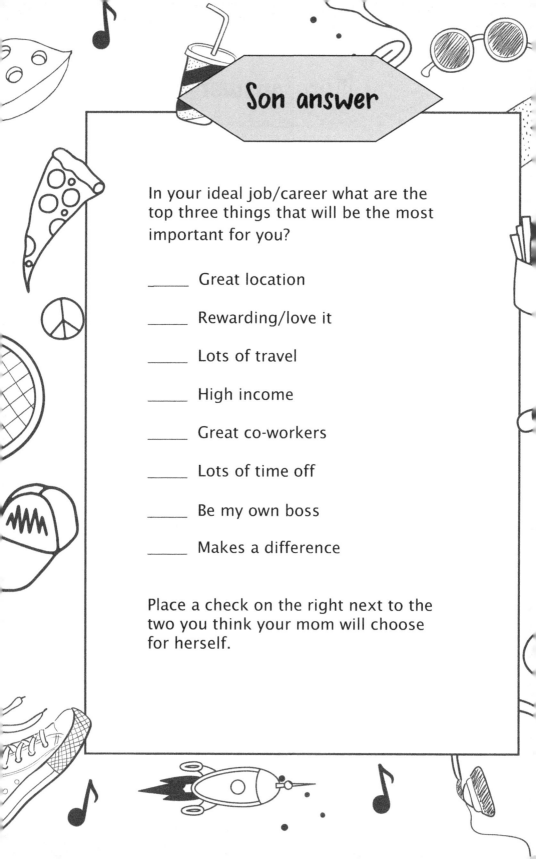

Son answer

In your ideal job/career what are the top three things that will be the most important for you?

_____ Great location

_____ Rewarding/love it

_____ Lots of travel

_____ High income

_____ Great co-workers

_____ Lots of time off

_____ Be my own boss

_____ Makes a difference

Place a check on the right next to the two you think your mom will choose for herself.

We answer/discuss

Mom, have you achieved the things you chose? Have they changed over time?

_____

_____

_____

_____

_____

_____

_____

_____

_____

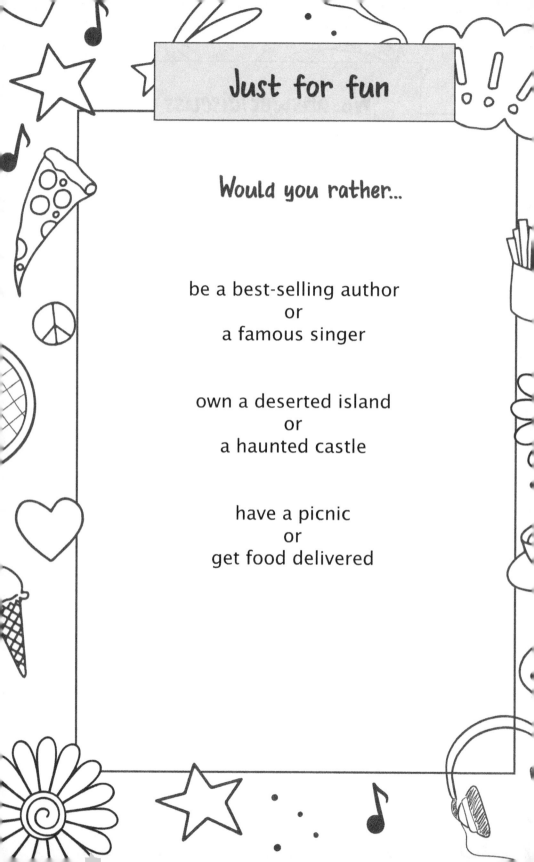

Just for fun

Would you rather...

be a best-selling author
or
a famous singer

own a deserted island
or
a haunted castle

have a picnic
or
get food delivered

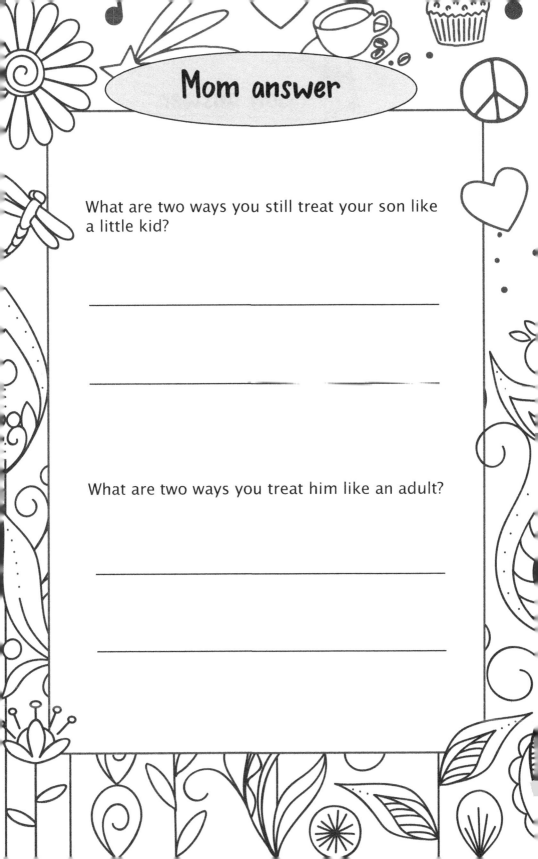

Mom answer

What are two ways you still treat your son like a little kid?

_____

_____

What are two ways you treat him like an adult?

_____

_____

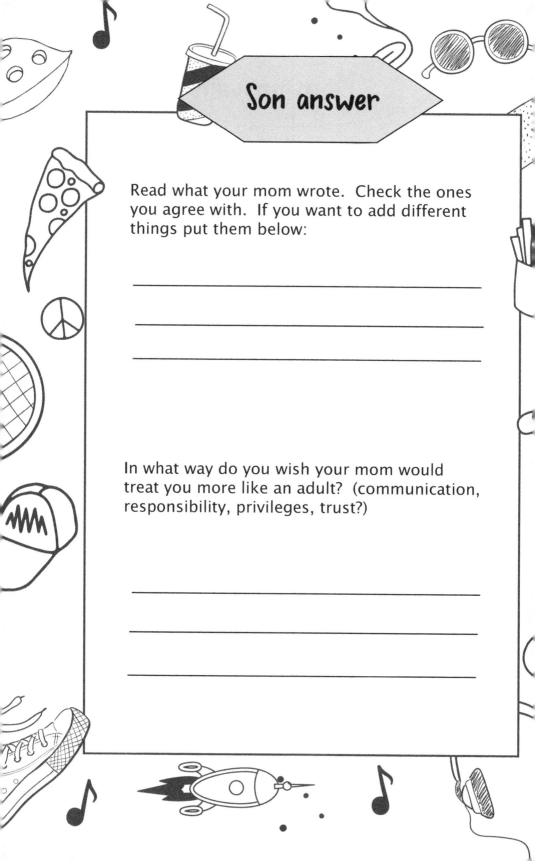

Son answer

Read what your mom wrote. Check the ones you agree with. If you want to add different things put them below:

_____

_____

_____

In what way do you wish your mom would treat you more like an adult? (communication, responsibility, privileges, trust?)

_____

_____

_____

We answer/discuss

Discuss if responsibilities and privileges should be earned by actions or by age. Have they been predetermined?

_____

_____

_____

_____

_____

_____

_____

_____

_____

Just for fun

Dots and Boxes

Take turns connecting 2 dots by drawing a line between them. When you draw the last line of a single box, put your initial in it, and make the next move. Player with the most boxes wins.

Mom answer

What do you think is better of the choices below?

	Winning $20	Finding $20	
	City	Country	
	Surprises	Planned events	
	Extra Credit	Curve	
	Running	Swimming	
	Spring	Fall	

What do you think your son will choose for himself?

	Winning $20	Finding $20	
	City	Country	
	Surprises	Planned events	
	Extra Credit	Curve	
	Running	Swimming	
	Spring	Fall	

What do you think is better of the choices below?

	Winning $20	Finding $20	
	City	Country	
	Surprises	Planned events	
	Extra Credit	Curve	
	Running	Swimming	
	Spring	Fall	

What do you think your mom will choose for herself?

	Winning $20	Finding $20	
	City	Country	
	Surprises	Planned events	
	Extra Credit	Curve	
	Running	Swimming	
	Spring	Fall	

We answer/discuss

If you found a suitcase full of money in the woods, what would you do? Would it make a difference if it contained $50, $500, $50,000 or 5 million dollars?

_____

_____

_____

_____

_____

_____

_____

_____

_____

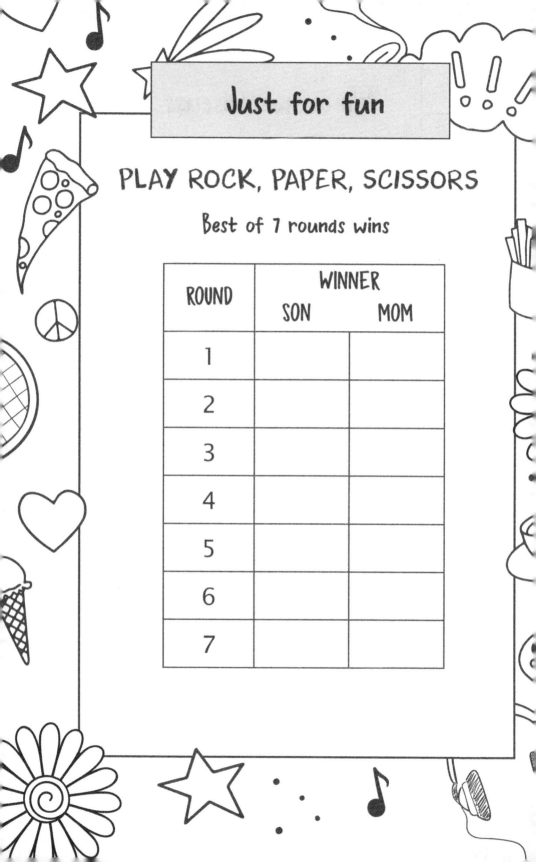

Just for fun

PLAY ROCK, PAPER, SCISSORS

Best of 7 rounds wins

ROUND	WINNER	
	SON	MOM
1		
2		
3		
4		
5		
6		
7		

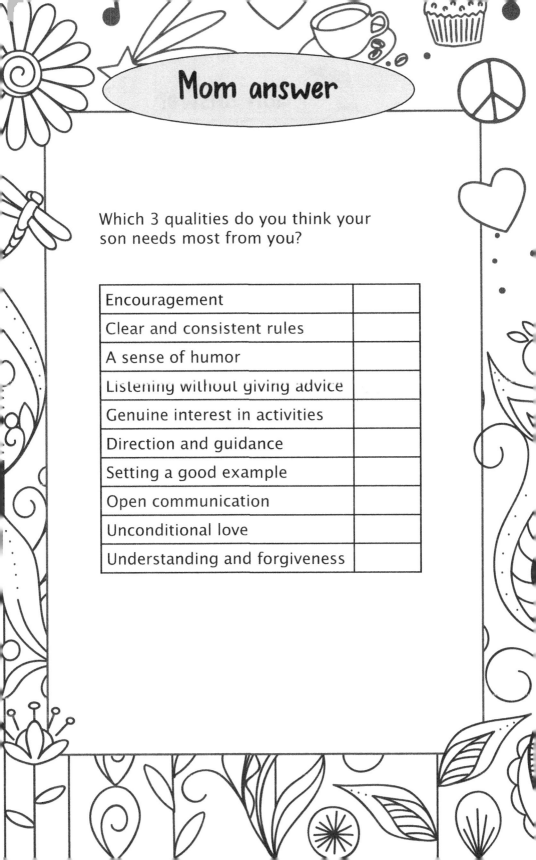

Mom answer

Which 3 qualities do you think your son needs most from you?

Encouragement	
Clear and consistent rules	
A sense of humor	
Listening without giving advice	
Genuine interest in activities	
Direction and guidance	
Setting a good example	
Open communication	
Unconditional love	
Understanding and forgiveness	

Pick the top 2 qualities you need most from your mom:

Encouragement	
Clear and consistent rules	
A sense of humor	
Listening without giving advice	
Genuine interest in activities	
Direction and guidance	
Setting a good example	
Open communication	
Unconditional love	
Understanding and forgiveness	

We answer/discuss

Discuss or write about ways you could make
your top choices happen.

_____

_____

_____

_____

_____

_____

_____

_____

_____

_____

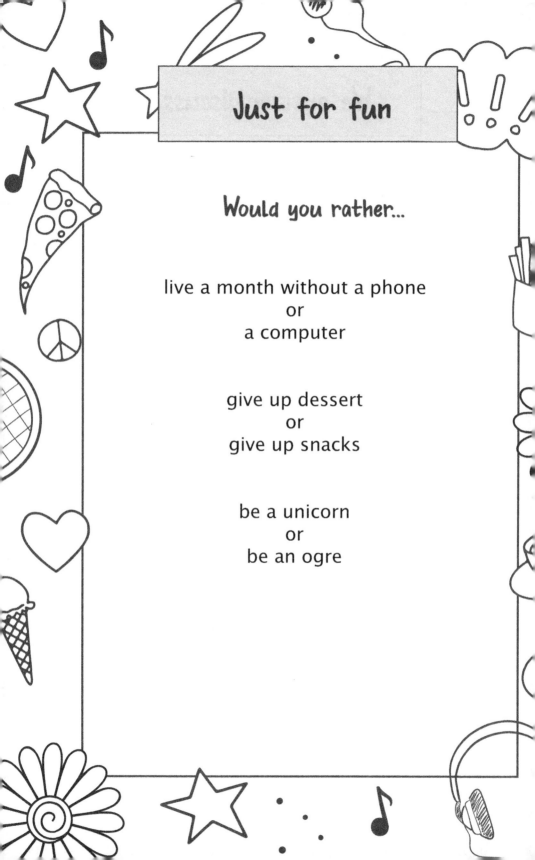

Just for fun

Would you rather...

live a month without a phone
or
a computer

give up dessert
or
give up snacks

be a unicorn
or
be an ogre

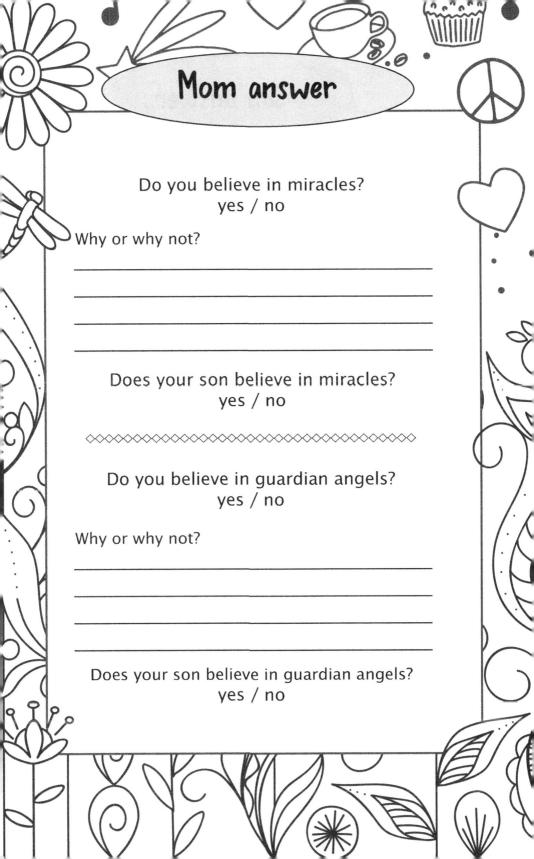

Mom answer

Do you believe in miracles?
yes / no

Why or why not?

_____

_____

_____

_____

Does your son believe in miracles?
yes / no

Do you believe in guardian angels?
yes / no

Why or why not?

_____

_____

_____

_____

Does your son believe in guardian angels?
yes / no

Son answer

Do you believe in miracles?
yes / no

Why or why not?

_____
_____
_____
_____

Does your mom believe in miracles?
yes / no

◇◇◇◇◇◇◇◇◇◇◇◇◇◇◇◇◇◇◇◇◇◇◇◇◇◇◇◇◇◇◇◇◇◇◇

Do you believe in guardian angels?
yes / no

Why or why not?

_____
_____
_____
_____

Does your mom believe in guardian angels?
yes / no

We answer/discuss

Have you ever or do you know someone who has had a personal experience with either? Did you believe them? Which one do you hope exists more?

_____

_____

_____

_____

_____

_____

_____

_____

_____

Just for fun

Dots and Boxes

Take turns connecting 2 dots by drawing a line between them. When you draw the last line of a single box, put your initial in it, and make the next move. Player with the most boxes wins.

Mom answer

Your son will be living in one of these for the summer. Which will be his top 2 choices?

What would be your top 3 choices?

	Son	Mom
an RV		
a yurt		
a tiny house		
a deluxe tree house		
a sailboat		
a tent		
a houseboat		

You will be living in one of these for the summer. Which are your top 3 choices?

What would be your mom's top 2 choices?

	Me	Mom
an RV		
a yurt		
a tiny house		
a deluxe tree house		
a sailboat		
a tent		
a houseboat		

We answer/discuss

Which one of you deals better with change? Is the idea of living in a different place exciting or stressful?

_____

_____

_____

_____

_____

_____

_____

_____

_____

Just for fun

Dots and Boxes

Take turns connecting 2 dots by drawing a line between them. When you draw the last line of a single box, put your initial in it, and make the next move. Player with the most boxes wins.

Mom answer

CONGRATULATIONS...
You are now a member of one of the
following...
Check your first choice and what you
think your son will choose.

You   Son

____   Seal Team 6   ____

____   Knights of the   ____
            Round Table

____   Olympic Team   ____

____   Supreme Court   ____

CONGRATULATIONS...
You are now a member of one of the following...
Check your first choice and what you think your mom will choose.

You   Mom

____   Seal Team 6   ____

____   Knights of the   ____
            Round Table

____   Olympic Team   ____

____   Supreme Court   ____

We answer/discuss

Discuss why you made the choices you did.
Were you surprised by each others answer?

_____

_____

_____

_____

_____

_____

_____

_____

_____

_____

Just for fun

Mom answer

In what two ways are you and your son the most alike?

_____

_____

_____

_____

In what two ways are you and your son the most different?

_____

_____

_____

_____

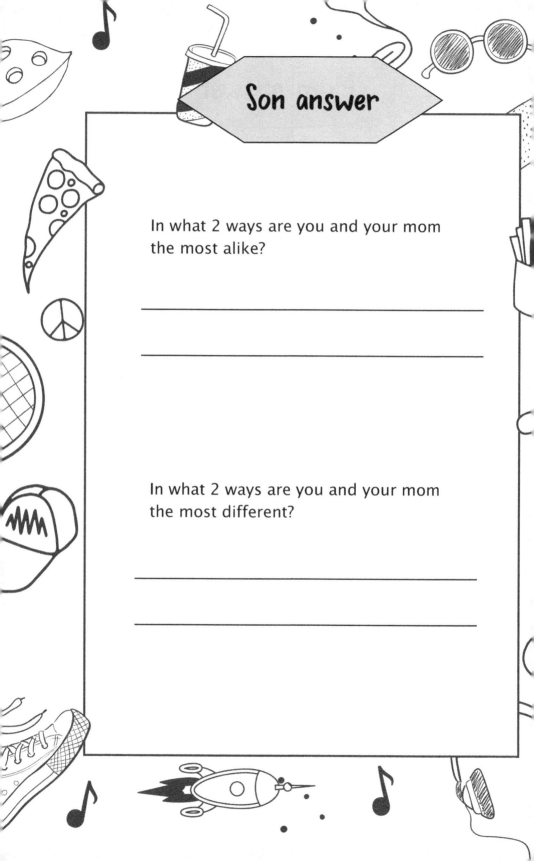

Son answer

In what 2 ways are you and your mom the most alike?

_____

_____

In what 2 ways are you and your mom the most different?

_____

_____

We answer/discuss

Do you work better together as a team or is it better if you divide and attack tasks separately? At school/work do you prefer working by yourself or in a group?

_____

_____

_____

_____

_____

_____

_____

_____

_____

Just for fun

PLAY ROCK, PAPER, SCISSORS

Best of 7 rounds wins

ROUND	WINNER	
	SON	MOM
1		
2		
3		
4		
5		
6		
7		

Mom answer

Which of you .... more?
(check one for each row)

	Mom	Son
daydreams		
complains		
relaxes		
farts		
finds happiness in little things		
judges other people		
gives advice		
laughs		
worries		
talks		

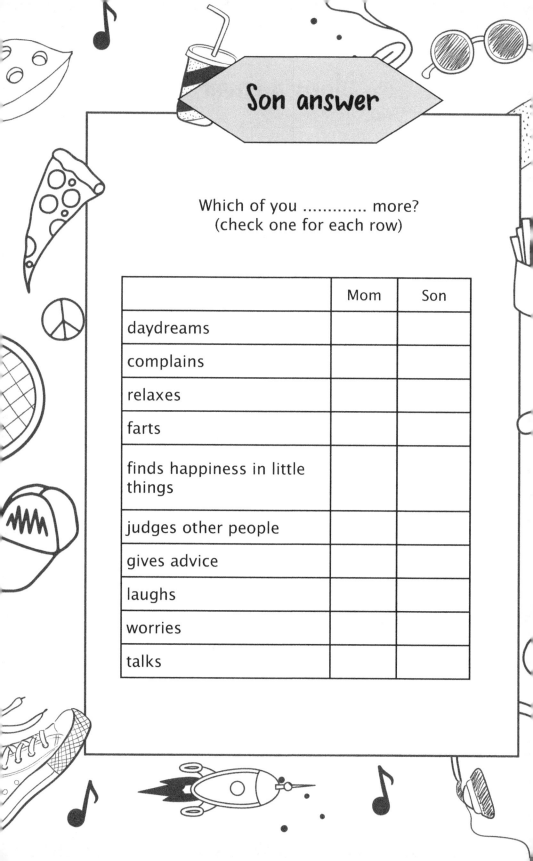

Son answer

Which of you .... more?
(check one for each row)

	Mom	Son
daydreams		
complains		
relaxes		
farts		
finds happiness in little things		
judges other people		
gives advice		
laughs		
worries		
talks		

We answer/discuss

Did you agree? Which would be good for both of you to do more of? Less of?

_____

_____

_____

_____

_____

_____

_____

_____

Just for fun

Would you rather...

stop time
or
speed up time

have wings
or
have gills

be the oldest
or
be the youngest

Mom answer

So...it turns out you get a super power on your next birthday that will last exactly one month. What do you hope it is?

_____ mind control

_____ invisibility

_____ super strength & speed

_____ ability to fly

_____ healing

How will you use it?

_____

_____

_____

What will your son choose?

_____ mind control   _____ invisibility

_____ super strength & speed

_____ ability to fly   _____ healing

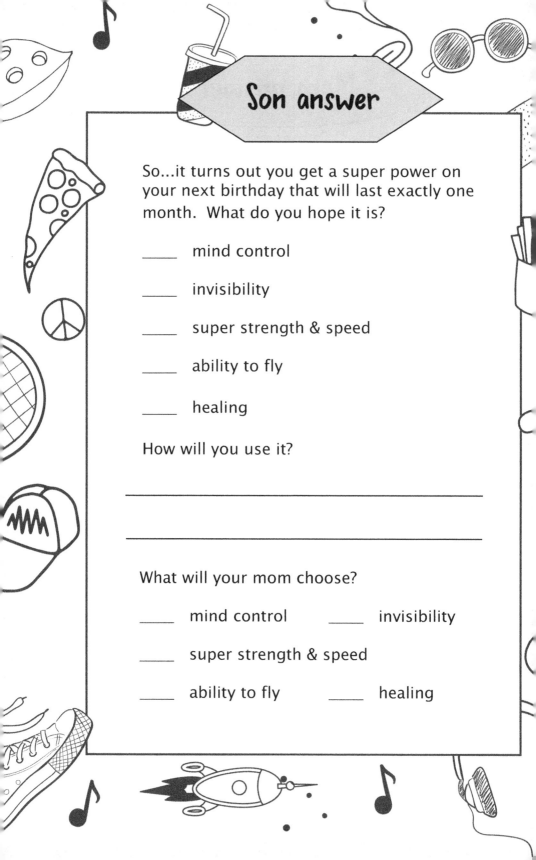

Son answer

So...it turns out you get a super power on your next birthday that will last exactly one month. What do you hope it is?

____ mind control

____ invisibility

____ super strength & speed

____ ability to fly

____ healing

How will you use it?

_____

_____

What will your mom choose?

____ mind control   ____ invisibility

____ super strength & speed

____ ability to fly   ____ healing

We answer/discuss

What if you got to keep the power, but it would shorten your life by 10 years. Would it be worth it? If everyone in the world had one of these powers what would be the best choice for all?

_____

_____

_____

_____

_____

_____

_____

_____

_____

_____

Just for fun

Dots and Boxes

Take turns connecting 2 dots by drawing a line between them. When you draw the last line of a single box, put your initial in it, and make the next move. Player with the most boxes wins.

Mom answer

Do you believe in karma?
yes / no

Why or why not?

_____
_____
_____
_____

Does your son believe in karma?
yes/no

◇◇◇◇◇◇◇◇◇◇◇◇◇◇◇◇◇◇◇◇◇◇◇◇◇◇◇◇◇◇◇◇◇◇

Do you believe in love at first sight?
yes / no

Why or why not?

_____
_____
_____
_____

Does your son believe in love at
first sight?
yes/no

Son answer

Do you believe in karma?
yes / no

Why or why not?

_____
_____
_____
_____

Does your mom believe in karma?
yes/no

◇◇◇◇◇◇◇◇◇◇◇◇◇◇◇◇◇◇◇◇◇◇◇◇◇◇◇◇◇◇◇◇

Do you believe in love at first sight?
yes / no

Why or why not?

_____
_____
_____
_____

Does your mom believe in love at first
sight?
yes/no

We answer/discuss

Have you ever or do you know someone who has had a personal experience with either? Did you believe them? Which one do you hope exists more?

_____

_____

_____

_____

_____

_____

_____

_____

_____

Just for fun

Mom answer

You just won a time travel trip!

Do you want to go:

_____ to the past

_____ to the future

what period of time in the past or how far into the future?

_____

_____

What would you want to see or do?

_____

_____

Do you think your son will want to go:

_____ to the past

_____ to the future

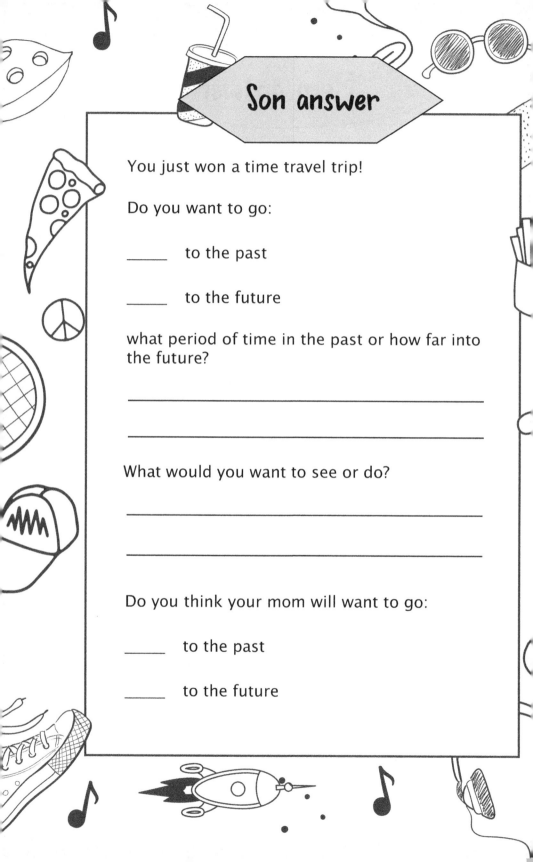

Son answer

You just won a time travel trip!

Do you want to go:

_____ to the past

_____ to the future

what period of time in the past or how far into the future?

_____

_____

What would you want to see or do?

_____

_____

Do you think your mom will want to go:

_____ to the past

_____ to the future

We answer/discuss

Who would you want to meet? Where would you like to go together? If you had to be there permanently, would you make the same choice?

_____

_____

_____

_____

_____

_____

_____

_____

_____

PLAY ROCK, PAPER, SCISSORS

Best of 7 rounds wins

ROUND	WINNER	
	SON	MOM
1		
2		
3		
4		
5		
6		
7		

Mom answer

Your son just won a **Vacation Home** that he can use every weekend. The perfect place would be...(check one in each group)

located

_____ on the oceanfront

_____ in the mountains

_____ by a lake

with a great view of the

_____ sunrise

_____ sunset

There would be plenty of

_____ outdoor activities

_____ indoor activities

and lots of

_____ quiet time

_____ parties

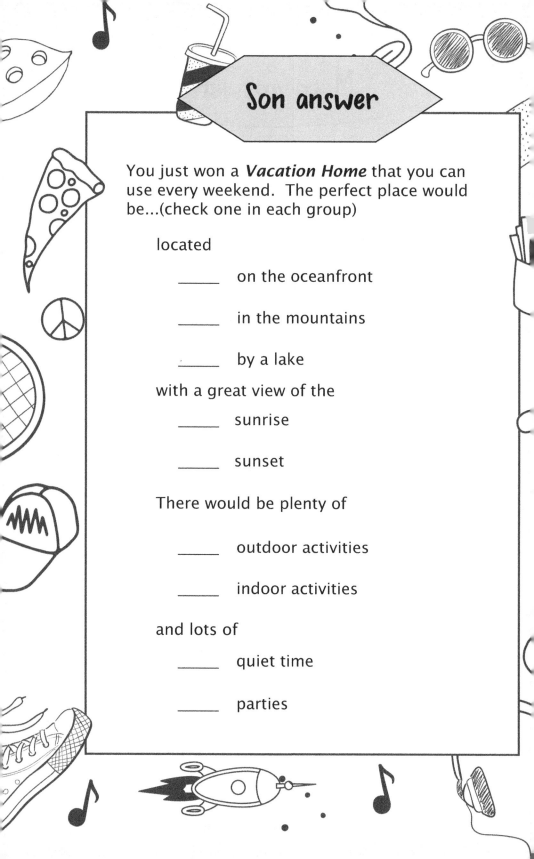

Son answer

You just won a *Vacation Home* that you can use every weekend. The perfect place would be...(check one in each group)

located

_____ on the oceanfront

_____ in the mountains

_____ by a lake

with a great view of the

_____ sunrise

_____ sunset

There would be plenty of

_____ outdoor activities

_____ indoor activities

and lots of

_____ quiet time

_____ parties

We answer/discuss

Would you want to live there permanently? Why or why not?

_____

_____

_____

_____

_____

_____

_____

_____

_____

_____

Mom – draw your sons favorite

fast food

sport to play

dessert

animal

Son – draw your moms favorite

fast food

sport to play

dessert

animal

Mom answer

Check 3 things you hope your son knows:

____ how much I love him

____ what a great person I think he is

____ how much I worry about him

____ how much I believe in him

____ how much I trust him

____ how special he is

____ how much I expect of him

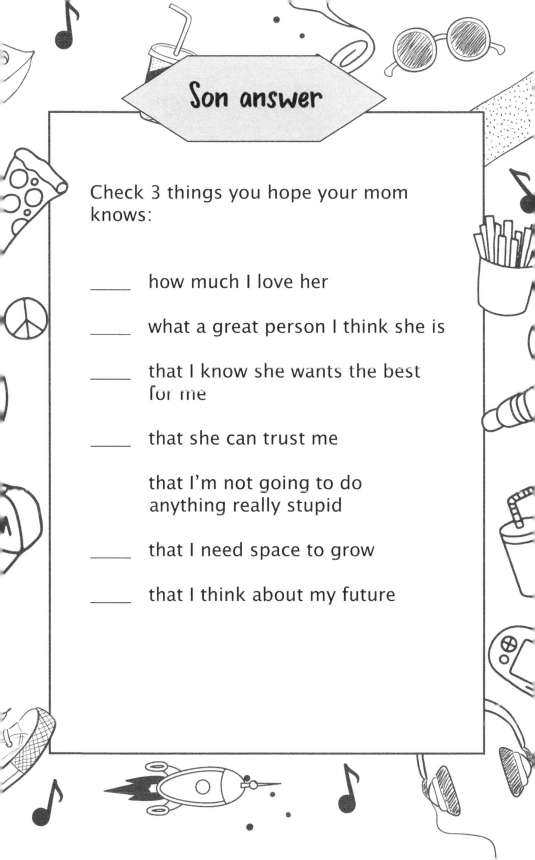

Check 3 things you hope your mom knows:

____ how much I love her

____ what a great person I think she is

____ that I know she wants the best for me

____ that she can trust me

that I'm not going to do anything really stupid

____ that I need space to grow

____ that I think about my future

Mom answer

Question:

_____

_____

_____

Answer:

_____

_____

_____

_____

_____

_____

_____

_____

_____

_____

_____

_____

_____

_____

_____

_____

Son answer

Question:
_____
_____
_____

Answer:
_____
_____
_____
_____
_____
_____
_____
_____
_____
_____
_____
_____
_____
_____
_____
_____
_____
_____

Mom answer

Question:

_____
_____
_____

Answer:

_____
_____
_____
_____
_____
_____
_____
_____
_____
_____
_____
_____
_____
_____
_____
_____
_____

Son answer

Question:

_____

_____

_____

Answer:

_____

_____

_____

_____

_____

_____

_____

_____

_____

_____

_____

_____

_____

_____

_____

_____

_____

Mom answer

Question:

_____

_____

_____

Answer:

_____

_____

_____

_____

_____

_____

_____

_____

_____

_____

_____

_____

_____

_____

_____

_____

Son answer

Question:
_____
_____
_____

Answer:
_____
_____
_____
_____
_____
_____
_____
_____
_____
_____
_____
_____
_____
_____
_____
_____
_____
_____
_____
_____

Mom answer

Question:
_____
_____
_____

Answer:
_____
_____
_____
_____
_____
_____
_____
_____
_____
_____
_____
_____
_____
_____
_____
_____
_____

Son answer

Question:

_____

_____

_____

Answer:

_____

_____

_____

_____

_____

_____

_____

_____

_____

_____

_____

_____

_____

_____

_____

_____

Mom answer

Question:
_____
_____
_____

Answer:
_____
_____
_____
_____
_____
_____
_____
_____
_____
_____
_____
_____
_____
_____
_____

Son answer

Question:

_____

_____

_____

Answer:

_____

_____

_____

_____

_____

_____

_____

_____

_____

_____

_____

_____

_____

_____

_____

_____

_____

_____

Mom answer

Question:

_____
_____
_____

Answer:

_____
_____
_____
_____
_____
_____
_____
_____
_____
_____
_____
_____
_____
_____
_____
_____
_____

Son answer

Question:
_____
_____
_____

Answer:
_____
_____
_____
_____
_____
_____
_____
_____
_____
_____
_____
_____
_____
_____
_____
_____
_____
_____

Mom answer

Question:
_____
_____
_____

Answer:
_____
_____
_____
_____
_____
_____
_____
_____
_____
_____
_____
_____
_____
_____
_____
_____
_____
_____

Son answer

Question:

_____

_____

_____

Answer:

_____

_____

_____

_____

_____

_____

_____

_____

_____

_____

_____

_____

_____

_____

_____

_____

_____

Made in the USA
Monee, IL
20 November 2022

18138967R00072